AF606830

The Empowered Wife

Workbook & Journal

Also by Laura Doyle

The Surrendered Wife
The Surrendered Single
Things Will Get as Good as You Can Stand
The Empowered Wife, Updated and Expanded Edition

The Empowered Wife

Workbook & Journal

A Guided Journey to
TRANSFORMING YOUR MARRIAGE
with the Six Intimacy Skills

Laura Doyle

***New York Times* Bestselling Author**

BenBella Books, Inc.
Dallas, TX

BenBella Books, Inc.
10440 N. Central Expressway
Suite 800
Dallas, TX 75231
benbellabooks.com
Send feedback to feedback@benbellabooks.com

BenBella is a federally registered trademark.

Printed in the United States of America
10 9 8 7 6 5 4 3 2 1

ISBN 9781637742396 (print)
ISBN 9781637742402 (ebook)

Editing by Alexa Stevenson
Copyediting by Lydia Choi
Proofreading by Michael Fedison
Text design and composition by Aaron Edmiston
Cover design by Sarah Avinger
Cover image © Adobe Stock / worldwide_stock
Printed by Lake Book Manufacturing

Contents

How to Use This Workbook and Journal

My book *The Empowered Wife* explains the Six Intimacy Skills™, formed from the exact phrases, mindset, and steps I gathered from women who had happy marriages and that I used to save my own marriage. They started a worldwide movement over twenty years ago and have transformed the lives of thousands of women and their families. With this workbook and journal, the timeless wisdom and power of the Intimacy Skills can transform you and your marriage too, one week at a time, while making you happier and more relaxed.

Using this workbook and guided journal is a great way to take action with the Intimacy Skills—and "action" is the magic word. You'll find powerful quotes here for inspiration and motivation, and questions to encourage self-reflection. I'm inviting you to take self-assessments and experiment with exercises.

You can start this journal anytime, and I invite you to use it in a way that's responsive to you. I'll prompt you to try specific activities, and you get to do them as you see fit for your situation. You'll have opportunities to express your desires in a way that inspires, create spouse-fulfilling prophecies, and visit your future self to hear about how everything went your way.

Some of the exercises will feel very awkward or even scary. That's normal. I invite you to stretch but not tear. The Intimacy Skills are tools, not rules, that you can use in all of your interactions with your husband regarding parenting, finances, physical intimacy, in-laws, vacations, and holidays. Think of each exercise as an experiment, or something you're trying on in the dressing room to see if it fits. If it works for you like it has for the thousands of women before you who have experimented with these methods, then great! But if it's not a fit, I trust you as the expert of your own life. Only you know what's best for you.

There's no rush to get through this workbook in a particular time frame. When you feel motivated to develop yourself, desire progress in your marriage, or want to connect with yourself and honor your feelings and desires, this workbook and journal will help you find peace, restore your hope, and reinforce your new practices so that they become habits.

The exercises are a lot of fun! They're all about you, what you're thankful for, what you want more of, and what you enjoy. The invitations to action are for your transformation and delight—and to bring out the best in your husband and everyone else in your life. If you're anything like me, you'll start to feel like you have superpowers as you become more skilled.

Now more than ever, the world needs women like you who are committed to making their marriages shiny and amazing. Thank you for your courage and determination to make your marriage last and thrive!

INTIMACY SKILL #1

Replenish Your Spirit with Self-Care

The first indispensable step to improving your marriage is practicing the art of replenishing your spirit by *making your happiness a priority*, including having frivolous fun. If you've ever felt stuck waiting for your husband to make you happy, this is the key to rediscovering your delight and enjoyment, which is critical for making your marriage last and thrive.

Make Your Self-Care List

Twenty things that are frivolous fun and make me feel happy are:

1. ______________________________

2. ______________________________

3. ______________________________

4. ______________________________

5. ______________________________

6. ______________________________

7. ______________________________

8. ______________________________

9. ______________________________

10. ______________________________

11. ______________________________

12. ______________________________

13. ______________________________

14. ______________________________

15. ______________________________

16. ______________________________

17. ______________________________

18. ______________________________

19. ______________________________

20. ______________________________

My self-care activities (or non-activities) for today were:

1. ______________________________

2. ______________________________

3. ______________________________

Three things I will do for my self-care tomorrow and when I will do them:

1. ______________________ *Time:* ________

2. ______________________ *Time:* ________

3. ______________________ *Time:* ________

Evaluate Your Happiness

When you find yourself annoyed at your husband or wanting him to change, one powerful question to ask yourself is "How is my self-care?"

Rate your self-care on a scale of 1 to 10, with 1 meaning that you're not happy at all and 10 meaning that you're feeling ridiculously happy: ______

If your self-care is at a 6 or above, well done on making yourself happy!

If your self-care is at a 5 or below, what else could you do to make yourself happy right now?

1. ______________________________
2. ______________________________
3. ______________________________
4. ______________________________

Make Your Desires List

One way to know how to make yourself happy is to identify and honor your desires by writing them down.

What are the things you're longing for, big and small? Include desires you're afraid to say out loud because they're scary or you think you'll lose something else. Maybe you want a new car but you also want to keep expenses down to pay off debt. You can desire both! (Hot tip: Your desires don't actually have to be realistic. Maybe you want to quit your job even though your family depends on the income.)

Remember to focus on the outcomes, not how they happen. And don't worry if your desires change later—that's a woman's prerogative.

1. ______________________________

2. ______________________________

3. ______________________________

4. ______________________________

5. ______________________________

6. ______________________________

7. ______________________________

8. ______________________________

9. ______________________________

10. ______________________________

11. ______________________________

12. ______________________________

13. ______________________________

14. ______________________________

15. ______________________________

16. ______________________________

Express Your Desires in a Way that Inspires Him

Think of something that you have repeatedly asked your husband/boyfriend to do—or stop doing.

I've asked my husband/boyfriend to: ______________________

____

____

How do you usually phrase this request? __________________

____

____

His usual response/reaction is: ________________________

____

____

My usual response/reaction to his is: ____________________

____

____

This leaves me feeling: ______________________________

____

____

What is your desire? What is the end result you would like? (Think about the final outcome you really want, not what you want him to do.) ______________________________

____

____

____

How could you phrase this as a pure desire without criticism, expectation, or complaining? ______________________________

____

____

____

What other desires could you express in a way that inspires your husband?

1. ______________________________
2. ______________________________
3. ______________________________

Before you express a desire, check to see if it has the word "you" in it (which would make it a means of control rather than a pure desire). Double-check for the hidden "you" in words such as "family," "us," "we," and "together."

Write out your desire, starting with "I would love . . ." followed by the final outcome:

I would love ______________________________

Look for opportunities to express this desire over the next forty-eight hours and then write about the experience. How did you feel bringing it up? How did he respond? __________

____

____

Make Your Friends List

Every marriage needs encouragement and support. List your friends and family who are standing *for* your marriage. Who can you share openly with about your wins and challenges in your journey of making your marriage last and thrive?

1. ______________________________
2. ______________________________
3. ______________________________
4. ______________________________
5. ______________________________

INTIMACY SKILL #2

Respect

Respecting your husband means honoring his choices for himself rather than dismissing, criticizing, contradicting, or trying to improve him. You won't always agree with your husband, but treating him with respect requires you to listen to him regardless. Expecting the best outcome from his decisions is critical for a peaceful and passionate marriage.

What Attracted You to Your Husband?

Remember when you first fell for your man? What was it that you liked and admired about him back then? List as many things as you can think of. (Write in the margins if there isn't enough room!)

1. ____________________

2. ____________________

3. ____________________

4. ____________________

5. ____________________

6. ____________________

7. ____________________

8. ____________________

9. ____________________

10. ____________________

Check Your Side of the Street

Consider the conflicts or breakdowns in your relationship. How might you have contributed to them? Your husband is responsible for his own behavior, of course, but if you focus just on what *you* might have liked to do better or differently, what, specifically, would you change? Have there been things you've said or done that weren't reflective of your best self?

1. ____

____

____

____

____

2. ____

____

____

____

____

3. ____

____

____

____

Experiment with Apologizing for Being Disrespectful

What specific words or actions that may have been disrespectful are you willing to apologize for to keep your side of the street clean?

____

____

____

____

____

____

____

Write out an apology using the formula for apologizing for being disrespectful:

I apologize for being disrespectful when I _______________

____

____

____

The end! If you decide to deliver this apology, resist the temptation to justify, defend, or comment further.

Experiment with Saying "I Hear You"

For thirty minutes, listen to your husband (or anyone else you'd like to practice with) by saying only "uh-huh" or "I hear you."

Describe your experience—how you felt doing it and how he reacted:

____

____

____

____

____

____

Experiment with Saying "Whatever You Think"

I invite you to experiment with the phrase "Whatever you think" when you're tempted to help your husband make decisions.

Over the next twenty-four hours, listen for your opportunity to refer him back to his own thinking with this powerful cheat phrase. Maybe he's asking how long he should cook the vegetables. Or if he should get a new job. Or if he should buy a new belt. Or if he should take the freeway. Or if he can give the kids ice cream. Every one of those questions is an opportunity for you to show that you trust him—even if you don't feel so trusting right now—by saying, "Whatever you think."

It's shorthand for "You're so capable and smart. I'm sure you'll make a good decision."

The time you don't want to use this phrase, however, is when he's asking about your desires. If he asks, "Do you want the vegetables crispy or soft?" you can take advantage of the opportunity to state your desires instead.

Write about your experience experimenting with the phrase "Whatever you think." What were the issues at hand? How did you feel about using this phrase? How did he respond?

Resist the Bait

Sometimes your husband will say something that seems like an invitation to an old dance you no longer want to do, whether it's intentional or not. There are lots of ways to RSVP "not attending," such as using humor, asking a rhetorical question, responding with "I don't know," or simply saying, "That's a good question!"

Write down a recurring situation where you feel baited:

____

____

____

Create a game plan for how you'll respond the next time you hear this particular bait: ___________________________

____

____

____

Write about your experience with resisting the bait: _______

____

____

____

INTIMACY SKILL #3

Relinquish Inappropriate Control

Control and intimacy are opposites, just like light and dark. So you can choose intimacy or control (at least the illusion of it), but you can't have both. If you choose control, intimacy will disappear. If you choose intimacy, you'll have to leave control at the door.

Trying to control your husband is not only ineffective and harmful to the intimacy between you—it's also exhausting. Practicing the Intimacy Skills to give up inappropriate control will not only improve your marriage but will also leave you with more energy.

What Are You Doing That You Could Stop?

What chores, errands, or other responsibilities are you doing that you wish you didn't have to do or that make you feel exhausted or resentful?

	Yes/No/ Maybe
1. ______________________________ ______________________________	______
2. ______________________________ ______________________________	______
3. ______________________________ ______________________________	______

Yes/No/
Maybe

4. ____ ______

____

5. ____ ______

____

6. ____ ______

____

Are any of the items on your list something you do to help your husband with his own responsibilities or a shared responsibility that you've taken on? Write "yes," "no," or "maybe" next to each one.

Do Less to Get More

Are you willing to experiment with relinquishing something from your list above?

Yes No Not yet

Would it make sense to formulate and deliver a simple "I can't" statement about it (i.e., "I can't pack your lunch," "I can't do your expense report," "I can't manage the bills," or "I can't pick you up tomorrow")? If so, write your "I can't" statement here:

____

____

____

____

Is it more appropriate to simply stop doing it (i.e., straightening his desk, picking up his clothes, making his doctor's appointments)?

____

____

____

____

What kinds of self-care could you engage in with the extra time and energy you'd gain from relinquishing this responsibility?

____

____

____

____

Ten Ways to Control Your Husband (None of These Work!)

These are some of the common ways I tried to control my husband, often without realizing that I was acting on fear. Put a check mark next to the ones that you identify with:

- ☐ Making helpful suggestions, like "You should diversify your portfolio" or "You should call your mom."
- ☐ Speaking on his behalf.
- ☐ Making decisions for him, like how much to contribute to his retirement or which clothes to get rid of in the closet.
- ☐ Shooting him disapproving looks and rolling my eyes.
- ☐ Asking leading questions (i.e., "Is that what you're going to eat for lunch?" "Do you have to leave so early to get there?" or "Does that shirt go with those pants?").
- ☐ Announcing that "we" need to go to counseling.
- ☐ Telling him how I would do things.
- ☐ Criticizing him to help him finally understand the error of his ways.
- ☐ Undoing and redoing things he's just done.
- ☐ Walking on eggshells so he won't get upset.

Find the Fear Underneath the Control

Think about something in your marriage that you want to control. What is it that you wish your husband would change?

Whether you want your husband to stop being so harsh with the kids, to help out more with chores, or to cut down on his drinking, write it down. If there's more than one thing, that's fine. Once you've written down what you're tempted to control, go through the following exercises:

Think about what your fear is that has you wanting to control what he does. What are you afraid will happen if you don't control him?

____

____

____

____

____

Is your fear realistic? (Some of mine were not that realistic, but that didn't stop me from acting on them!)

Yes No

Have your efforts to control him been working? (Or has it been like trying to tell the ocean to be still?)

Yes No

Is controlling him worth the loss of intimacy that you will experience? (Sometimes, for me, the answer to this is yes! But not very often anymore.)

Yes No

Remember: Only you know these answers because you are the expert on your own life.

INTIMACY SKILL #4

Receive, Receive, Receive!

Men are fundamentally attracted to the feminine mind, body, and spirit, and there is nothing more feminine than being receptive. Receiving graciously will make you more feminine, attractive, and confident.

Being a good receiver means that you smile and say "thank you" when you get gifts, compliments, help, or special treatment.

How Well Do You Receive?

1. Compliments

Imagine that someone says, "Your hair looks so pretty." Your hair is not especially styled, colored, or even clean. How would you respond?

____

____

____

____

____

2. Help

Imagine that you're moving chairs at work and a colleague offers to help you. You know that this is your job, not theirs. How would you respond?

____

____

____

____

3. Gifts

Imagine that a friend has given you a gift for your birthday, and you weren't expecting it. How would you respond?

____

____

____

____

4. Apologies

Imagine that a friend is late in meeting you for lunch, and when they arrive, they say, "I'm sorry I was late." How would you respond?

____

____

____

____

Think of a time when you did not receive graciously. What was holding you back?

____

____

____

Was it worth the loss of intimacy that you might have had in that moment with the giver?

Yes No

When it comes to receiving graciously, I have the most trouble with:

- ☐ Compliments
- ☐ Gifts
- ☐ Help
- ☐ Apologies

But I'm most gracious when receiving:

- ☐ Compliments
- ☐ Gifts
- ☐ Help
- ☐ Apologies

Practice receiving graciously by writing down what you're given. Did you reject or dismiss what was being offered? Or did you receive graciously by saying "thank you" and smiling?

What I Received:	How I Responded:
1. ______________	*1.* ______________
2. ______________	*2.* ______________
3. ______________	*3.* ______________
4. ______________	*4.* ______________
5. ______________	*5.* ______________
6. ______________	*6.* ______________
7. ______________	*7.* ______________
8. ______________	*8.* ______________
9. ______________	*9.* ______________
10. ______________	*10.* ______________

INTIMACY SKILL #5

Reveal Your Heart with Vulnerability

Being vulnerable means opening yourself up and being undefended, which can feel uncomfortable and awkward but is essential for intimacy.

Sometimes confused with weakness, vulnerability requires courage, and it includes acknowledging your limits out loud, expressing tender emotions, and even letting your authentic tears show at times.

Vulnerability is not only attractive; it's also necessary for that incredible, indescribable feeling of being loved just the way you are by someone who knows you well. There's nothing quite like it, and it really is worth risking everything to have it.

Say, "Ouch!"

Over the next twenty-four hours, look for an opportunity to say "Ouch!" and nothing else when you feel mad or hurt. "Ouch!" is best said in the moment that you feel mad or hurt rather than afterward.

It may be very tempting to go into an explanation about why you're saying "Ouch!"—especially if the person you say it to throws out bait like "What does that mean?" But for the purpose of this exercise, try staying quiet. You can always explain yourself later if this approach doesn't serve you. Also, I don't recommend this approach if you're feeling hurt or mad about something someone else *didn't* do, even if they said they would.

At first, you might see these opportunities going by in the rearview mirror, which can be frustrating. But in my experience, that's still progress because it means you're noticing those situations in retrospect, and that's part of the process.

Describe a situation where you felt mad or hurt:

Describe the response you got when you said, "Ouch!"

Important: How did you feel about yourself using this response?

If you felt like saying "Ouch!" didn't work, or if you got a negative response, replay the interaction in your head and ask yourself if your side of the street is clean. Did you say anything that could have been interpreted as criticism, control, or disrespect prior to feeling hurt or angry?

____

____

____

____

____

If you see anything on your side of the street that was critical, controlling, or disrespectful, consider how you might use the apology formula from Intimacy Skill #2: "I apologize for being disrespectful when I ______." What words go in the blank in this situation?

____

____

____

____

____

If it's helpful, reference the exercise on "Apologizing for Being Disrespectful" from Intimacy Skill #2 to deliver this apology.

Say, "I Can't"

What chores or activities are you doing that are making you feel overwhelmed or resentful, even if you think they're your responsibility (for example: working full-time, running errands, packing lunches, driving kids)?

1. ______________________________

2. ______________________________

3. ______________________________

4. ______________________________

5. ______________________________

Over the next forty-eight hours, consider saying "I can't" regarding one of these activities to acknowledge your own limits as a mere mortal woman and to give your husband the opportunity to be your hero.

The activity I will say "I can't" about is:

____

____

____

____

____

What kind of response did you get from saying "I can't"?

How did you feel about saying "I can't"?

The Smile Campaign

Over the next three days, consider proactively smiling at your husband whenever you see him as a way of being your happiest self and to show him that you're happy to see him.

What happened when you smiled at your husband?

Hop Off the Fence

Are you currently on the fence about your marriage? Does part of you want to stay and part of you want to go? What is stopping you from getting off the fence?

What would be possible for your marriage if you went all in on it?

Make Yourself Available for Physical Intimacy

Recommended: Complete the exercises in the "Intimacy Skill #2: Respect" section before you try this exercise.

If physical intimacy has gone missing and you want to restore it, consider flirting with your husband over the next three days. You might compliment him, tell him how amorous you're feeling, or dress to impress.

How will you flirt with your man?

____

____

____

____

It will take some courage to do this exercise! Over the next three days, to feel desired and amazing, make yourself available for physical intimacy rather than initiating it, even if it's been a while and you feel very awkward and vulnerable.

What are your desires around physical intimacy that would make it more enjoyable for you? Do you want a massage, music, a bubble bath, role-playing, toys, or something else? Write down your desires.

1. ______________________________

____

2. ____

3. ____

4. ____

5. ____

Which desire will you express to your husband?

Borrow His Brain for Your Problem

Think of a challenge you're facing. Do you have a tough decision to make or a problem to solve? Is something in your life feeling burdensome? It doesn't have to be anything big. Consider asking your husband if you can borrow his brain to help solve your challenge.

Write down a few things that you would love to solve:

1. ____
____

2. ____
____

3. ____
____

In the next three days, present one of these challenges to your husband by using the phrase "Can I borrow your brain? I would love to solve this challenge I have . . ." and then describing it. Try to use the "expressing your desires" language of "I would love . . ." as much as possible during this exercise.

How did your husband respond to you borrowing his brain?

____

____

INTIMACY SKILL #6

Refocus Your View with Gratitude

Gratitude is the most powerful of the Six Intimacy Skills because it does double duty: It changes your perspective, and it makes those around you feel appreciated, allowing them to respond to you better.

Putting on a new pair of grateful perspectacles can dramatically transform your experiences. Your husband and everyone else will respond to you better when you're leading with gratitude.

List Twenty-Two Gratitudes for Your Husband

I'm grateful for these things about my husband:

1. ______________________________

2. ______________________________

3. ______________________________

4. ______________________________

5. ______________________________

6. ______________________________

7. ______________________________

8. ______________________________

9. ______________________________

10. ______________________________

11. ______________________________

12. ______________________________

13. ______________________________

14. ______________________________

15. ______________________________

16. ______________________________

17. ______________________________

18. ______________________________

19. ______________________________

20. ______________________________

21. ______________________________

22. ______________________________

Express Three Gratitudes a Day

Three things I can thank my husband for today are:

1. ______________________________

2. ______________________________

3. ______________________________

Drop and Do Ten

Gratitude is a powerful way to put a stop to Needless Emotional Turmoil (NET for short). It's also a great way to shift your focus from an experience you don't want to have to creating the experience you do want to have.

What are ten things you're grateful for that also prove that your Needless Emotional Turmoil is truly needless?

1. ______________________________

2. ______________________________

3. ______________________________

4. ______________________________

5. ______________________________

6. ______________________________

7. ______________________________

8. ______________________________

9. ______________________________

10. ______________________________

Create a Spouse-Fulfilling Prophecy

Briefly write down your biggest complaint about your marriage:

____

____

____

____

____

This complaint is also a negative Spouse-Fulfilling Prophecy—which you probably have lots of evidence to support.

Flip the complaint into the experience you *want* to be having, which may be the opposite. Write your new, positive Spouse-Fulfilling Prophecy here, even if it sounds completely detached from reality:

____

____

____

____

____

What evidence is there that you are, in fact, having the experience you want with your husband (instead of the one you don't want to have)? Look for ten examples, big or small.

1. ____

____

2. ____

____

3. ____

____

4. ____

____

5. ____

____

6. ____

____

7. ____

____

8. ____

____

9. ____

____

10. ____

____

Express Three Gratitudes a Day for Seven Days

Consider expressing three gratitudes every day for a week, either verbally or in writing.

Day 1 Gratitudes

1. ______________________________

____

2. ______________________________

____

3. ______________________________

____

Day 2 Gratitudes

1. ______________________________

____

2. ______________________________

____

3. ______________________________

____

Day 3 Gratitudes

1. ____

____

2. ____

____

3. ____

____

Day 4 Gratitudes

1. ____

____

2. ____

____

3. ____

____

Day 5 Gratitudes

1. ______________________________

____

2. ______________________________

____

3. ______________________________

____

Day 6 Gratitudes

1. ______________________________

____

2. ______________________________

____

3. ______________________________

____

Day 7 Gratitudes

1. ______________________________

____

2. ______________________________

____

3. ______________________________

____

Write about your experience when you expressed your appreciation to your husband. How did you feel? How did he respond? Was there a shift in you or in your relationship?

____

____

____

____

____

The 30-Day Relationship Revitalization Challenge

The magic of the Six Intimacy Skills starts when you take action, and this 30-Day Relationship Revitalization Challenge is designed to give you a simple structure to kick-start the practices that will help you rediscover your hope, exercise your power, and restore your dignity.

There's nothing hard about this challenge (it includes having lots of fun!), but it will take some focus and energy, like everything in life that's worthwhile. Try to get plenty of rest each night and devote just a few minutes each day to incorporating the suggestions.

By the end of the challenge, you'll feel different, and you'll *be* different—and so will your marriage! You'll also have established some new habits that will serve you well as you continue to make your marriage last and thrive.

Day 1

Do something frivolous and fun to make yourself ridiculously happy. Then do something else that you like even more. Then do one more thing that brings you joy. If you can't stop smiling, you'll know you've done this step well.

Repeat these instructions every day of the challenge.

Day 2–Day 7

Create a running list of all the frivolous, fun things that you like to do.

Day 3

Notice that your happiness does not depend upon your man and what he does or doesn't do.

Day 4

Chat with a woman who gets you—a girlfriend, your sister, or your mom. Tell her you're on day four of a thirty-day plan for revitalizing your relationship. Tell her how it's going so far. Talk about everything in the world.

Day 5

Get some solitude—even if it's only for fifteen minutes.

Day 6

Write down the three fun things you did today. Ask yourself how happy you are. If you're not happy yet, do something else for frivolous fun until you are.

Day 7

Decline to do something that would be exhausting or make you resentful, even if you feel guilty about not doing it. Say, "I can't." Rest up for the happy week ahead.

Day 8

Be the Goddess of Fun and Light today—for the whole day. Start a disco in the kitchen. Wear sexy shoes or a hat. Smile at your husband. Laugh at his jokes. Sing at the top of your lungs. Have no expectations except to have fun.

Day 9

Think of something you want to control about your husband—something that bugs you or seems unacceptable to you. Next time it comes up and he says he's going to do the very thing that you want to control, say to him, "Whatever you think"—or, even better, "Whatever you think—I trust you." After all, you've already tried telling him not to do it, and that didn't work. Why not experiment with showing him that you trust his decisions and see what happens?

Day 10

Spend an hour listening to your husband by saying only "I hear you" or "uh-huh." Instead of reacting to what he says, consider just bearing witness. Give him the gift of being heard and understood. Notice how much more he has to say than usual.

Day 11

Recall something you've said to your husband that offended him, and then tell him: "I apologize for being disrespectful when I . . ." Fill in the blank with what you said. Notice how he glows when you say those words.

Day 12

Take stock of everything you appreciate about your husband. Write down at least ten good qualities.

Day 13

Read yesterday's list of good qualities to yourself.

Day 14

Pick one thing from Day 12's list and tell your husband how grateful you are for that one thing.

Day 15

Give yourself a gold star for your progress so far. You're halfway there! What changes have you noticed in yourself? What changes do you notice in your relationship?

Day 16

Focus on saying "thank you" to all the compliments you get today—not just from your man but from everyone. No arguing—just smile sweetly and say, "Thanks."

Day 17

Accept all the help that you're offered—to move the chairs, to take the groceries to the car, to clean up after the party—and accept it graciously, even if it feels uncomfortable.

Day 18

Think of a problem you have that's not related to your relationship. Say to your man, "Can I borrow your brain? I'm trying to solve this problem . . ." Let him help you. If his solution isn't quite what you want, keep explaining what you want. See what he has to say.

Day 19

For the whole day, focus on not interrupting your man. When he's speaking, stop what you're doing, put down your phone, and give him your attention. What do you notice that you hadn't before?

Day 20

Spend some time contemplating your desires. What do you want? Make a list. Make it long.

Day 21

Take something from yesterday's list of desires and say it out loud, starting with "I would love . . ."

Day 22

Think of something you wish your husband was more of: tidier, romantic, ambitious, funny, attentive. Just pick one thing. Today, look for evidence that he *is* that thing, even if it's small.

Day 23

Find more evidence that your guy is the positive thing you want him to be.

Day 24

Find still more evidence that your man is exceptionally gifted in the quality that you picked on Day 22.

Day 25

Tell your husband how grateful you are that he's tidy, romantic, ambitious, funny, or attentive, even if it feels like a huge stretch. It's okay—you have several days' worth of evidence.

Day 26

Thank your husband for three things that he does—like taking out the trash, working hard to support the family, or making the coffee. Tell your friend, mom, or sister how much you appreciate that he does those things.

Day 27

Thank your husband for three more things. Also, look for ways that you may have been disrespectful recently and apologize using the phrase from Day 11 if appropriate.

Day 28

Thank your husband for another three things, and express a desire from your Day 20 list out loud.

Day 29

Make yourself available for physical intimacy. Send him a flirtatious signal that you're not expecting anything—just hoping.

Day 30

Fill yourself up with frivolous fun and thank your husband for making you ridiculously happy for all these years. Reflect on how dignified, confident, and peaceful you feel.

You can repeat the entire challenge as often as you like to keep your relationship playful, passionate, and fun.

The Connection Framework

The Six Intimacy Skills™ are the first pillar of the Connection Framework™. Having the right information is a great start, but the key to transformation is applying that information, which happens best with the other three pillars.

The second pillar of the Connection Framework is having a like-minded community of women to practice the Skills with.

The third pillar is having a Certified Laura Doyle Relationship Coach to help you see what's in your blind spot.

The fourth pillar is being able to pass on what you've learned to someone else.

These four elements provide the information, inspiration, and motivation that have helped thousands of women make their marriages last and thrive!

What Will Help You Succeed?

The Six Intimacy Skills will likely feel uncomfortable or awkward when you first start practicing them. The other pillars of the Connection Framework will provide inspiration and support to help you keep implementing them.

Which of the Six Intimacy Skills have you experimented with?

- ☐ Self-Care
- ☐ Respect
- ☐ Relinquishing Inappropriate Control

- ☐ Receiving
- ☐ Vulnerability
- ☐ Gratitude

Which has been the most helpful for you so far?

____

____

____

____

Which has been the hardest to reach for?

____

____

____

____

Now that you have the first pillar, which of the other three pillars would help you on your journey of making your marriage last and thrive?

- ☐ Find your community
- ☐ Work with a Certified Laura Doyle Relationship Coach
- ☐ Pay forward what you've learned

Find Your Community

To mingle with like-minded women who also value a lasting, thriving marriage and will stand for yours too, join my free **Adored Wife Group** by visiting **www.LauraDoyle.org/group**. It's completely confidential, safe, and full of inspiration for wives.

Work with a Certified Laura Doyle Relationship Coach

Do you desire the support of a Certified Laura Doyle Relationship Coach? Do you want just a couple of private sessions, to be part of a group coaching experience, or to have the dedicated support of one coach over several months? Write out your specific desire using the formula for expressing your desires in a way that inspires, and then say it out loud.

I would love ______________________________

____

____

____

Another way to honor your desires is to share them with someone else. Who will you share your desires with? Remember that you don't have to know *how* your desire will be fulfilled to honor the final outcome that you want:

1. ______________________________

2. ______________________________

3. ______________________________

How would having a Certified Laura Doyle Relationship Coach support your vision for your marriage?

____

____

____

Pay Forward What You've Learned

Who do you know that may be struggling in their marriage?

1. ______________________________

2. ______________________________

3. ______________________________

Even if your marriage isn't all that you want it to be, you can still inspire someone else by sharing your experience. What have you learned about marriage that could benefit someone else?

____

____

____

Visit Your Future Self

“Imagination is more important than knowledge.”

—Albert Einstein

A great way to stay inspired with practicing the Six Intimacy Skills is to get in touch with your future self so you can get a glimpse of how well everything will turn out in your marriage. (Spoiler alert: You end up feeling desired, taken care of, and special!)

It's one year from now. And I have *great* news for you: Everything went your way. Everything! It's been an incredibly exciting year because your dreams have been coming true—and now things are so good, you can barely stand it.

I invite you to capture this vision in writing, using the following questions as inspiration or prompts to fill in the details for yourself:

- Have you and your husband been having deep conversations?
- Are you feeling desired and adored?
- Has he been telling you that he loves you?
- Are you snuggling on the couch or in bed?
- Are you taking a trip together?
- Did he just give you a present that feels really personal, sentimental, or meaningful?
- Did he tell you how beautiful you are and then make a pass at you?
- Are you getting a new home together?
- How are your kids impacted by their parents being so in love?
- Are you growing your family?

Write down what your future self is experiencing:

In your future, how are your relationships with your extended family—your in-laws, for example—or those between your husband and your family?

____

____

____

____

What projects or activities are you currently excited about and having fun with?

____

____

____

____

How is your future self feeling? Do you feel secure? Happy? Loved? Elated? Joyful? Grateful?

____

____

____

____

____

If you knew for sure that this future you're envisioning will come to be, how would it change the way you show up in your relationship today?

____

____

____

____

____

____

You may hear a voice in your head arguing against this beautiful vision you've just created, trying to discourage you by saying that it's never going to happen. It's like a mean, miserable person is trying to squash your imagination and your dreams!

But can you find some evidence that your vision is actually already coming true? Can you find at least three things that prove your vision is possible? Do you see even small things that contribute to your hope and your determination to create this vision? List them here:

1. ____________________________________

2. ____________________________________

3. ____________________________________

Think about how important this inner conversation is. You're writing in this workbook because of your decision to end world divorce in the most significant way possible—by making your marriage last and thrive. And that is creating more love in the world. You're making yourself a beacon of hope for what is possible in marriage, and others will start to see that light in you. Doubt will try to douse that light. Doubt will try to obscure that possibility. But you're choosing your faith.

I want to acknowledge you for articulating your vision for your marriage and writing it down—and choosing to focus on it even when you feel afraid. I admire that very much! The world needs more women like you who make their marriage a priority.

The Empowered Wife Guided Journal

The Empowered Wife Guided Journal creates space for you to reflect on and then rewrite your own marriage story. It'll help you create a habit of choosing to focus on the things that serve you well instead of getting stuck fretting about the things that don't.

Here's an example of how to use this daily habit former:

How are you winning with the Six Intimacy Skills?

1. I went for a walk to make myself happy.

2. My husband brought home sushi after I expressed my desire in a way that inspires.

3.

Self-Care

1. Played a word game on my phone
2. Played volleyball
3. Slept in
4.
5.

Rate your happiness on a scale of 1 to 10: 5

If you are at a 6 or above, well done on making yourself happy!

If 5 or below, what else could you do to make yourself happy right now?

Walk around the block

Talk to a friend or my sister

Watch a funny video

Listen to a podcast or music

How do you feel (use a feeling word, like "mad," "sad," "bad," "glad," "afraid," "tired," or "hungry")? Hungry

What do you want? To have a meal with John

Desires

1. Go for a bike ride
2. New purse
3. To be faster in volleyball
4. Finish this week's podcast
5. More flexibility in my legs

Desires to Express

I would love to eat watermelon tonight.

Receiving

What You Received:	How You Responded:
1. *Help from plumber*	1. *Thank you*
2. *Compliment from friend (oops!)*	2. *Argued with her*
3. *Tea from John*	3. *Thank you*
4.	4.
5.	5.

Gratitude

Daily Gratitude for Your Husband:	Expressed to Him?
1. *Picking up supplies*	*Not yet*
2. *Making me tea*	*Yes*
3. *Handling investment*	*Yes*
4.	
5.	

Spouse-Fulfilling Prophecy

You make me feel safe and taken care of.

Evidence That Your Spouse-Fulfilling Prophecy Is True

1. Prepares all the accounting for taxes
2. Pays all the bills
3. offers to bring home whatever I want for dinner daily
4.
5.

Day 1

How are you winning with the Six Intimacy Skills?

1. ______________________________

____

2. ______________________________

____

3. ______________________________

____

Self-Care

1. ______________________________
2. ______________________________
3. ______________________________
4. ______________________________
5. ______________________________

Rate your happiness on a scale of 1 to 10: ______

If you are at a 6 or above, well done on making yourself happy!

If 5 or below, what else could you do to make yourself happy right now?

____

____

____

____

____

How do you feel (use a feeling word, like "mad," "sad," "bad," "glad," "afraid," "tired," or "hungry")? ______________

What do you want? ______________

Desires

1. ______________________________
2. ______________________________
3. ______________________________
4. ______________________________
5. ______________________________

Desires to Express

___

___

___

Receiving

What You Received:	How You Responded:
1. ______	1. ______
2. ______	2. ______
3. ______	3. ______
4. ______	4. ______
5. ______	5. ______

Gratitude

Daily Gratitude for Your Husband:	Expressed to Him?
1. ______	______
2. ______	______
3. ______	______
4. ______	______
5. ______	______

Spouse-Fulfilling Prophecy

____

____

____

____

____

Evidence That Your Spouse-Fulfilling Prophecy Is True

1. ____
2. ____
3. ____
4. ____
5. ____

Day 2

How are you winning with the Six Intimacy Skills?

1. ______________________________

____

2. ______________________________

____

3. ______________________________

____

Self-Care

1. ______________________________
2. ______________________________
3. ______________________________
4. ______________________________
5. ______________________________

Rate your happiness on a scale of 1 to 10: ______

If you are at a 6 or above, well done on making yourself happy!

If 5 or below, what else could you do to make yourself happy right now?

____

____

____

____

____

How do you feel (use a feeling word, like "mad," "sad," "bad," "glad," "afraid," "tired," or "hungry")? ______________

What do you want? ______________

Desires

1. ______________________________
2. ______________________________
3. ______________________________
4. ______________________________
5. ______________________________

Desires to Express

____

____

____

Receiving

What You Received:	How You Responded:
1. ________________	*1.* ________________
2. ________________	*2.* ________________
3. ________________	*3.* ________________
4. ________________	*4.* ________________
5. ________________	*5.* ________________

Gratitude

Daily Gratitude for Your Husband:	Expressed to Him?
1. ____________________________	______
2. ____________________________	______
3. ____________________________	______
4. ____________________________	______
5. ____________________________	______

Spouse-Fulfilling Prophecy

____

____

____

____

____

Evidence That Your Spouse-Fulfilling Prophecy Is True

1. ____

2. ____

3. ____

4. ____

5. ____

Day 3

How are you winning with the Six Intimacy Skills?

1. ______________________________

____

2. ______________________________

____

3. ______________________________

____

Self-Care

1. ______________________________
2. ______________________________
3. ______________________________
4. ______________________________
5. ______________________________

Rate your happiness on a scale of 1 to 10: ______

If you are at a 6 or above, well done on making yourself happy!

If 5 or below, what else could you do to make yourself happy right now?

____

____

____

____

____

How do you feel (use a feeling word, like "mad," "sad," "bad," "glad," "afraid," "tired," or "hungry")? ______________

What do you want? ______________

Desires

1. ______________
2. ______________
3. ______________
4. ______________
5. ______________

Desires to Express

____

____

____

Receiving

What You Received:	How You Responded:
1. ____________	1. ____________
2. ____________	2. ____________
3. ____________	3. ____________
4. ____________	4. ____________
5. ____________	5. ____________

Gratitude

Daily Gratitude for Your Husband:	Expressed to Him?
1. ________________________	______
2. ________________________	______
3. ________________________	______
4. ________________________	______
5. ________________________	______

Spouse-Fulfilling Prophecy

____

____

____

____

____

Evidence That Your Spouse-Fulfilling Prophecy Is True

1. ____
2. ____
3. ____
4. ____
5. ____

Day 4

How are you winning with the Six Intimacy Skills?

1. ____________________________________

____

2. ____________________________________

____

3. ____________________________________

____

Self-Care

1. ____________________________________
2. ____________________________________
3. ____________________________________
4. ____________________________________
5. ____________________________________

Rate your happiness on a scale of 1 to 10: ______

If you are at a 6 or above, well done on making yourself happy!

If 5 or below, what else could you do to make yourself happy right now?

____

____

____

____

____

How do you feel (use a feeling word, like "mad," "sad," "bad," "glad," "afraid," "tired," or "hungry")? ______________

What do you want? ______________________

Desires

1. ______________________
2. ______________________
3. ______________________
4. ______________________
5. ______________________

Desires to Express

____

____

____

Receiving

What You Received:	How You Responded:
1. ________________	*1.* ________________
2. ________________	*2.* ________________
3. ________________	*3.* ________________
4. ________________	*4.* ________________
5. ________________	*5.* ________________

Gratitude

Daily Gratitude for Your Husband:	Expressed to Him?
1. ____________________________	______
2. ____________________________	______
3. ____________________________	______
4. ____________________________	______
5. ____________________________	______

Spouse-Fulfilling Prophecy

____

____

____

____

____

Evidence That Your Spouse-Fulfilling Prophecy Is True

1. ____

2. ____

3. ____

4. ____

5. ____

Day 5

How are you winning with the Six Intimacy Skills?

1. ____________________

____

2. ____________________

____

3. ____________________

____

Self-Care

1. ____________________
2. ____________________
3. ____________________
4. ____________________
5. ____________________

Rate your happiness on a scale of 1 to 10: ______

If you are at a 6 or above, well done on making yourself happy!

If 5 or below, what else could you do to make yourself happy right now?

____

____

____

____

____

How do you feel (use a feeling word, like "mad," "sad," "bad," "glad," "afraid," "tired," or "hungry")? ________________

What do you want? ____________________________

Desires

1. ____________________________________
2. ____________________________________
3. ____________________________________
4. ____________________________________
5. ____________________________________

Desires to Express

____

____

____

Receiving

What You Received:	How You Responded:
1. ________________	1. ________________
2. ________________	2. ________________
3. ________________	3. ________________
4. ________________	4. ________________
5. ________________	5. ________________

Gratitude

Daily Gratitude for Your Husband:	Expressed to Him?
1. ____________________________	_____
2. ____________________________	_____
3. ____________________________	_____
4. ____________________________	_____
5. ____________________________	_____

Spouse-Fulfilling Prophecy

____

____

____

____

____

Evidence That Your Spouse-Fulfilling Prophecy Is True

1. ______________________________________
2. ______________________________________
3. ______________________________________
4. ______________________________________
5. ______________________________________

Day 6

How are you winning with the Six Intimacy Skills?

1. ______________________________

____

2. ______________________________

____

3. ______________________________

____

Self-Care

1. ______________________________

2. ______________________________

3. ______________________________

4. ______________________________

5. ______________________________

Rate your happiness on a scale of 1 to 10: ______

If you are at a 6 or above, well done on making yourself happy!

If 5 or below, what else could you do to make yourself happy right now?

____

____

____

____

____

How do you feel (use a feeling word, like "mad," "sad," "bad," "glad," "afraid," "tired," or "hungry")? ____________________

What do you want? ______________________________

Desires

1. ____
2. ____
3. ____
4. ____
5. ____

Desires to Express

____

____

____

Receiving

What You Received:	How You Responded:
1. __________	*1.* __________
2. __________	*2.* __________
3. __________	*3.* __________
4. __________	*4.* __________
5. __________	*5.* __________

Gratitude

Daily Gratitude for Your Husband:	Expressed to Him?
1. ______________________	_____
2. ______________________	_____
3. ______________________	_____
4. ______________________	_____
5. ______________________	_____

Spouse-Fulfilling Prophecy

____

____

____

____

____

Evidence That Your Spouse-Fulfilling Prophecy Is True

1. ____
2. ____
3. ____
4. ____
5. ____

Day 7

How are you winning with the Six Intimacy Skills?

1. ______________________________

____

2. ______________________________

____

3. ______________________________

____

Self-Care

1. ______________________________
2. ______________________________
3. ______________________________
4. ______________________________
5. ______________________________

Rate your happiness on a scale of 1 to 10: ______

If you are at a 6 or above, well done on making yourself happy!

If 5 or below, what else could you do to make yourself happy right now?

____

____

____

____

____

How do you feel (use a feeling word, like "mad," "sad," "bad," "glad," "afraid," "tired," or "hungry")? ________________

What do you want? __________________________

Desires

1. ____________________________________

2. ____________________________________

3. ____________________________________

4. ____________________________________

5. ____________________________________

Desires to Express

____

____

____

Receiving

What You Received:	How You Responded:
1. ____________	1. ____________
2. ____________	2. ____________
3. ____________	3. ____________
4. ____________	4. ____________
5. ____________	5. ____________

Gratitude

Daily Gratitude for Your Husband:	Expressed to Him?
1. ________________________	______
2. ________________________	______
3. ________________________	______
4. ________________________	______
5. ________________________	______

Spouse-Fulfilling Prophecy

____

____

____

____

____

Evidence That Your Spouse-Fulfilling Prophecy Is True

1. ____________________________________
2. ____________________________________
3. ____________________________________
4. ____________________________________
5. ____________________________________

Day 8

How are you winning with the Six Intimacy Skills?

1. ______________________________

____

2. ______________________________

____

3. ______________________________

____

Self-Care

1. ______________________________
2. ______________________________
3. ______________________________
4. ______________________________
5. ______________________________

Rate your happiness on a scale of 1 to 10: ______

f you are at a 6 or above, well done on making yourself happy!

If 5 or below, what else could you do to make yourself happy right now?

____

____

____

____

____

How do you feel (use a feeling word, like "mad," "sad," "bad," "glad," "afraid," "tired," or "hungry")? ________________

What do you want? ______________________________

Desires

1. ____

2. ____

3. ____

4. ____

5. ____

Desires to Express

____

____

____

Receiving

What You Received:	How You Responded:
1. ________________	*1.* ________________
2. ________________	*2.* ________________
3. ________________	*3.* ________________
4. ________________	*4.* ________________
5. ________________	*5.* ________________

Gratitude

Daily Gratitude for Your Husband:	Expressed to Him?
1. ______________________________	_____
2. ______________________________	_____
3. ______________________________	_____
4. ______________________________	_____
5. ______________________________	_____

Spouse-Fulfilling Prophecy

____

____

____

____

____

Evidence That Your Spouse-Fulfilling Prophecy Is True

1. ____
2. ____
3. ____
4. ____
5. ____

Day 9

How are you winning with the Six Intimacy Skills?

1. ______________________________

____

2. ______________________________

____

3. ______________________________

____

Self-Care

1. ______________________________
2. ______________________________
3. ______________________________
4. ______________________________
5. ______________________________

Rate your happiness on a scale of 1 to 10: ______

If you are at a 6 or above, well done on making yourself happy!

If 5 or below, what else could you do to make yourself happy right now?

____

____

____

____

____

How do you feel (use a feeling word, like "mad," "sad," "bad," "glad," "afraid," "tired," or "hungry")? ____________________

What do you want? ______________________________

Desires

1. ______________________________________
2. ______________________________________
3. ______________________________________
4. ______________________________________
5. ______________________________________

Desires to Express

____

____

____

Receiving

What You Received:	How You Responded:
1. __________	1. __________
2. __________	2. __________
3. __________	3. __________
4. __________	4. __________
5. __________	5. __________

Gratitude

Daily Gratitude for Your Husband:	Expressed to Him?
1. ____________________	____
2. ____________________	____
3. ____________________	____
4. ____________________	____
5. ____________________	____

Spouse-Fulfilling Prophecy

____

____

____

____

____

Evidence That Your Spouse-Fulfilling Prophecy Is True

1. ____________________________________
2. ____________________________________
3. ____________________________________
4. ____________________________________
5. ____________________________________

Day 10

How are you winning with the Six Intimacy Skills?

1. ______________________________

____

2. ______________________________

____

3. ______________________________

____

Self-Care

1. ______________________________
2. ______________________________
3. ______________________________
4. ______________________________
5. ______________________________

Rate your happiness on a scale of 1 to 10: ______

If you are at a 6 or above, well done on making yourself happy!

If 5 or below, what else could you do to make yourself happy right now?

____

____

____

____

____

How do you feel (use a feeling word, like "mad," "sad," "bad," "glad," "afraid," "tired," or "hungry")? ______________

What do you want? ______________________

Desires

1. ______________________

2. ______________________

3. ______________________

4. ______________________

5. ______________________

Desires to Express

____

____

____

Receiving

What You Received:	How You Responded:
1. ____________	*1.* ____________
2. ____________	*2.* ____________
3. ____________	*3.* ____________
4. ____________	*4.* ____________
5. ____________	*5.* ____________

Gratitude

Daily Gratitude for Your Husband:	Expressed to Him?
1. ________________________	____
2. ________________________	____
3. ________________________	____
4. ________________________	____
5. ________________________	____

Spouse-Fulfilling Prophecy

____

____

____

____

____

Evidence That Your Spouse-Fulfilling Prophecy Is True

1. ____________________________________

2. ____________________________________

3. ____________________________________

4. ____________________________________

5. ____________________________________

Day 11

How are you winning with the Six Intimacy Skills?

1. ______________________________

____

2. ______________________________

____

3. ______________________________

____

Self-Care

1. ______________________________
2. ______________________________
3. ______________________________
4. ______________________________
5. ______________________________

Rate your happiness on a scale of 1 to 10: ______

If you are at a 6 or above, well done on making yourself happy!

If 5 or below, what else could you do to make yourself happy right now?

____

____

____

____

____

How do you feel (use a feeling word, like "mad," "sad," "bad," "glad," "afraid," "tired," or "hungry")? ______________

What do you want? ______________________

Desires

1. ______________________________
2. ______________________________
3. ______________________________
4. ______________________________
5. ______________________________

Desires to Express

____

____

____

Receiving

What You Received:	How You Responded:
1. ________________	1. ________________
2. ________________	2. ________________
3. ________________	3. ________________
4. ________________	4. ________________
5. ________________	5. ________________

Gratitude

Daily Gratitude for Your Husband:	Expressed to Him?
1. ____________________________	______
2. ____________________________	______
3. ____________________________	______
4. ____________________________	______
5. ____________________________	______

Spouse-Fulfilling Prophecy

____

____

____

____

____

Evidence That Your Spouse-Fulfilling Prophecy Is True

1. ____

2. ____

3. ____

4. ____

5. ____

Day 12

How are you winning with the Six Intimacy Skills?

1. ______________________________

   ____

2. ______________________________

   ____

3. ______________________________

   ____

Self-Care

1. ______________________________
2. ______________________________
3. ______________________________
4. ______________________________
5. ______________________________

Rate your happiness on a scale of 1 to 10: ______

f you are at a 6 or above, well done on making yourself happy!

If 5 or below, what else could you do to make yourself happy right now?

____

____

____

____

____

How do you feel (use a feeling word, like "mad," "sad," "bad," "glad," "afraid," "tired," or "hungry")? ________________

What do you want? ____________________________

Desires

1. ______________________________________

2. ______________________________________

3. ______________________________________

4. ______________________________________

5. ______________________________________

Desires to Express

____

____

____

Receiving

What You Received:	How You Responded:
1. __________	1. __________
2. __________	2. __________
3. __________	3. __________
4. __________	4. __________
5. __________	5. __________

Gratitude

Daily Gratitude for Your Husband:	Expressed to Him?
1. ____________________	____
2. ____________________	____
3. ____________________	____
4. ____________________	____
5. ____________________	____

Spouse-Fulfilling Prophecy

____

____

____

____

____

Evidence That Your Spouse-Fulfilling Prophecy Is True

1. ______________________________________
2. ______________________________________
3. ______________________________________
4. ______________________________________
5. ______________________________________

Day 13

How are you winning with the Six Intimacy Skills?

1. ______________________________

   ____

2. ______________________________

   ____

3. ______________________________

   ____

Self-Care

1. ______________________________
2. ______________________________
3. ______________________________
4. ______________________________
5. ______________________________

Rate your happiness on a scale of 1 to 10: ______

If you are at a 6 or above, well done on making yourself happy!

If 5 or below, what else could you do to make yourself happy right now?

____

____

____

____

____

How do you feel (use a feeling word, like "mad," "sad," "bad," "glad," "afraid," "tired," or "hungry")? ____________________

What do you want? ______________________________

Desires

1. ____
2. ____
3. ____
4. ____
5. ____

Desires to Express

____

____

____

Receiving

What You Received:	How You Responded:
1. ______	1. ______
2. ______	2. ______
3. ______	3. ______
4. ______	4. ______
5. ______	5. ______

Gratitude

Daily Gratitude for Your Husband:	Expressed to Him?
1. ______	______
2. ______	______
3. ______	______
4 ______	______
5. ______	______

Spouse-Fulfilling Prophecy

____

____

____

____

____

Evidence That Your Spouse-Fulfilling Prophecy Is True

1. ____
2. ____
3. ____
4. ____
5. ____

Day 14

How are you winning with the Six Intimacy Skills?

1. ____

____

2. ____

____

3. ____

____

Self-Care

1. ____
2. ____
3. ____
4. ____
5. ____

Rate your happiness on a scale of 1 to 10: ______

If you are at a 6 or above, well done on making yourself happy!

If 5 or below, what else could you do to make yourself happy right now?

____

____

____

____

____

How do you feel (use a feeling word, like "mad," "sad," "bad," "glad," "afraid," "tired," or "hungry")? ______________

What do you want? ______________

Desires

1. ______________________________

2. ______________________________

3. ______________________________

4. ______________________________

5. ______________________________

Desires to Express

____

____

____

Receiving

What You Received:	How You Responded:
1. ____________	1. ____________
2. ____________	2. ____________
3. ____________	3. ____________
4. ____________	4. ____________
5. ____________	5. ____________

Gratitude

Daily Gratitude for Your Husband:	Expressed to Him?
1. ____________________	______
2. ____________________	______
3. ____________________	______
4. ____________________	______
5. ____________________	______

Spouse-Fulfilling Prophecy

____

____

____

____

____

Evidence That Your Spouse-Fulfilling Prophecy Is True

1. ____________________________________
2. ____________________________________
3. ____________________________________
4. ____________________________________
5. ____________________________________

Day 15

How are you winning with the Six Intimacy Skills?

1. ____

____

2. ____

____

3. ____

____

Self-Care

1. ____
2. ____
3. ____
4. ____
5. ____

Rate your happiness on a scale of 1 to 10: ________

If you are at a 6 or above, well done on making yourself happy!

If 5 or below, what else could you do to make yourself happy right now?

____

____

____

____

____

How do you feel (use a feeling word, like "mad," "sad," "bad," "glad," "afraid," "tired," or "hungry")? ____________________

What do you want? __________________________________

Desires

1. ____

2. ____

3. ____

4. ____

5. ____

Desires to Express

____

____

____

Receiving

What You Received:	How You Responded:
1. ________________	*1.* ________________
2. ________________	*2.* ________________
3. ________________	*3.* ________________
4. ________________	*4.* ________________
5. ________________	*5.* ________________

Gratitude

Daily Gratitude for Your Husband:	Expressed to Him?
1. ______________________________	______
2. ______________________________	______
3. ______________________________	______
4. ______________________________	______
5. ______________________________	______

Spouse-Fulfilling Prophecy

____

____

____

____

____

Evidence That Your Spouse-Fulfilling Prophecy Is True

1. ____________________________________
2. ____________________________________
3. ____________________________________
4. ____________________________________
5. ____________________________________

Day 16

How are you winning with the Six Intimacy Skills?

1. ______________________________

____

2. ______________________________

____

3. ______________________________

____

Self-Care

1. ______________________________
2. ______________________________
3. ______________________________
4. ______________________________
5. ______________________________

Rate your happiness on a scale of 1 to 10: ______

If you are at a 6 or above, well done on making yourself happy!

If 5 or below, what else could you do to make yourself happy right now?

____

____

____

____

____

How do you feel (use a feeling word, like "mad," "sad," "bad," "glad," "afraid," "tired," or "hungry")? ______________

What do you want? ______________________

Desires

1. ______________________________

2. ______________________________

3. ______________________________

4. ______________________________

5. ______________________________

Desires to Express

____

____

____

Receiving

What You Received:	How You Responded:
1. ________________	1. ________________
2. ________________	2. ________________
3. ________________	3. ________________
4. ________________	4. ________________
5. ________________	5. ________________

Gratitude

Daily Gratitude for Your Husband:	Expressed to Him?
1. ____________________________	_____
2. ____________________________	_____
3. ____________________________	_____
4. ____________________________	_____
5. ____________________________	_____

Spouse-Fulfilling Prophecy

____

____

____

____

____

Evidence That Your Spouse-Fulfilling Prophecy Is True

1. ____
2. ____
3. ____
4. ____
5. ____

Day 17

How are you winning with the Six Intimacy Skills?

1. ______________________________

____

2. ______________________________

____

3. ______________________________

____

Self-Care

1. ______________________________
2. ______________________________
3. ______________________________
4. ______________________________
5. ______________________________

Rate your happiness on a scale of 1 to 10: ______

If you are at a 6 or above, well done on making yourself happy!

If 5 or below, what else could you do to make yourself happy right now?

____

____

____

____

____

How do you feel (use a feeling word, like "mad," "sad," "bad," "glad," "afraid," "tired," or "hungry")? __________________

What do you want? ______________________________

Desires

1. ____
2. ____
3. ____
4. ____
5. ____

Desires to Express

____

____

____

Receiving

What You Received:	How You Responded:
1. ________________	1. ________________
2. ________________	2. ________________
3. ________________	3. ________________
4. ________________	4. ________________
5. ________________	5. ________________

Gratitude

Daily Gratitude for Your Husband:	Expressed to Him?
1. ____________________________	______
2. ____________________________	______
3. ____________________________	______
4. ____________________________	______
5. ____________________________	______

Spouse-Fulfilling Prophecy

____

____

____

____

____

Evidence That Your Spouse-Fulfilling Prophecy Is True

1. ____________________________________

2. ____________________________________

3. ____________________________________

4. ____________________________________

5. ____________________________________

Day 18

How are you winning with the Six Intimacy Skills?

1. ____

____

2. ____

____

3. ____

____

Self-Care

1. ____

2. ____

3. ____

4. ____

5. ____

Rate your happiness on a scale of 1 to 10: ______

If you are at a 6 or above, well done on making yourself happy!

If 5 or below, what else could you do to make yourself happy right now?

____

____

____

____

____

How do you feel (use a feeling word, like "mad," "sad," "bad," "glad," "afraid," "tired," or "hungry")? ____________________

What do you want? ______________________________

Desires

1. ______________________________________
2. ______________________________________
3. ______________________________________
4. ______________________________________
5. ______________________________________

Desires to Express

____

____

____

Receiving

What You Received:	How You Responded:
1. ________________	1. ________________
2. ________________	2. ________________
3. ________________	3. ________________
4. ________________	4. ________________
5. ________________	5. ________________

Gratitude

Daily Gratitude for Your Husband:	Expressed to Him?
1. ______________________________	______
2. ______________________________	______
3. ______________________________	______
4. ______________________________	______
5. ______________________________	______

Spouse-Fulfilling Prophecy

____

____

____

____

____

Evidence That Your Spouse-Fulfilling Prophecy Is True

1. ____
2. ____
3. ____
4. ____
5. ____

Day 19

How are you winning with the Six Intimacy Skills?

1. ______________________________

____

2. ______________________________

____

3. ______________________________

____

Self-Care

1. ______________________________
2. ______________________________
3. ______________________________
4. ______________________________
5. ______________________________

Rate your happiness on a scale of 1 to 10: ______

If you are at a 6 or above, well done on making yourself happy!

If 5 or below, what else could you do to make yourself happy right now?

____

____

____

____

____

How do you feel (use a feeling word, like "mad," "sad," "bad," "glad," "afraid," "tired," or "hungry")? ________________

What do you want? ______________________________

Desires

1. ______________________________________

2. ______________________________________

3. ______________________________________

4. ______________________________________

5. ______________________________________

Desires to Express

____

____

____

Receiving

What You Received:	How You Responded:
1. ____________	1. ____________
2. ____________	2. ____________
3. ____________	3. ____________
4. ____________	4. ____________
5. ____________	5. ____________

Gratitude

Daily Gratitude for Your Husband:	Expressed to Him?
1. ____________________	______
2. ____________________	______
3. ____________________	______
4. ____________________	______
5. ____________________	______

Spouse-Fulfilling Prophecy

____

____

____

____

____

Evidence That Your Spouse-Fulfilling Prophecy Is True

1. ____
2. ____
3. ____
4. ____
5. ____

Day 20

How are you winning with the Six Intimacy Skills?

1. ______________________________

____

2. ______________________________

____

3. ______________________________

____

Self-Care

1. ______________________________
2. ______________________________
3. ______________________________
4. ______________________________
5. ______________________________

Rate your happiness on a scale of 1 to 10: ______

If you are at a 6 or above, well done on making yourself happy!

If 5 or below, what else could you do to make yourself happy right now?

____

____

____

____

____

How do you feel (use a feeling word, like "mad," "sad," "bad," "glad," "afraid," "tired," or "hungry")? ____________________

What do you want? ____________________________

Desires

1. ____

2. ____

3. ____

4. ____

5. ____

Desires to Express

____

____

____

Receiving

What You Received:

1. ______________
2. ______________
3. ______________
4. ______________
5. ______________

How You Responded:

1. ______________
2. ______________
3. ______________
4. ______________
5. ______________

Gratitude

Daily Gratitude for Your Husband:	Expressed to Him?
1. ______________________________	______
2. ______________________________	______
3. ______________________________	______
4. ______________________________	______
5. ______________________________	______

Spouse-Fulfilling Prophecy

____

____

____

____

____

Evidence That Your Spouse-Fulfilling Prophecy Is True

1. ____

2. ____

3. ____

4. ____

5. ____

Day 21

How are you winning with the Six Intimacy Skills?

1. ______________________________

____

2. ______________________________

____

3. ______________________________

____

Self-Care

1. ______________________________
2. ______________________________
3. ______________________________
4. ______________________________
5. ______________________________

Rate your happiness on a scale of 1 to 10: ______

If you are at a 6 or above, well done on making yourself happy!

If 5 or below, what else could you do to make yourself happy right now?

____

____

____

____

____

How do you feel (use a feeling word, like "mad," "sad," "bad," "glad," "afraid," "tired," or "hungry")? ____________________

What do you want? ______________________________

Desires

1. ____
2. ____
3. ____
4. ____
5. ____

Desires to Express

____

____

____

Receiving

What You Received:	How You Responded:
1. ________________	1. ________________
2. ________________	2. ________________
3. ________________	3. ________________
4. ________________	4. ________________
5. ________________	5. ________________

Gratitude

Daily Gratitude for Your Husband:	Expressed to Him?
1. ____________________________	_____
2. ____________________________	_____
3. ____________________________	_____
4. ____________________________	_____
5. ____________________________	_____

Spouse-Fulfilling Prophecy

____

____

____

____

____

Evidence That Your Spouse-Fulfilling Prophecy Is True

1. ____
2. ____
3. ____
4. ____
5. ____

Day 22

How are you winning with the Six Intimacy Skills?

1. ______________________________

____

2. ______________________________

____

3. ______________________________

____

Self-Care

1. ______________________________
2. ______________________________
3. ______________________________
4. ______________________________
5. ______________________________

Rate your happiness on a scale of 1 to 10: ______

If you are at a 6 or above, well done on making yourself happy!

If 5 or below, what else could you do to make yourself happy right now?

____

____

____

____

____

How do you feel (use a feeling word, like “mad,” “sad,” “bad,” “glad,” “afraid,” “tired,” or “hungry”)? ________________

What do you want? ____________________________

Desires

1. ____________________________________

2. ____________________________________

3. ____________________________________

4. ____________________________________

5. ____________________________________

Desires to Express

____

____

____

Receiving

What You Received:	How You Responded:
1. ________________	1. ________________
2. ________________	2. ________________
3. ________________	3. ________________
4. ________________	4. ________________
5. ________________	5. ________________

Gratitude

Daily Gratitude for Your Husband:	Expressed to Him?
1. ____________________________	_____
2. ____________________________	_____
3. ____________________________	_____
4. ____________________________	_____
5. ____________________________	_____

Spouse-Fulfilling Prophecy

____

____

____

____

____

Evidence That Your Spouse-Fulfilling Prophecy Is True

1. ____________________________________
2. ____________________________________
3. ____________________________________
4. ____________________________________
5. ____________________________________

Day 23

How are you winning with the Six Intimacy Skills?

1. ______________________________

____

2. ______________________________

____

3. ______________________________

____

Self-Care

1. ______________________________
2. ______________________________
3. ______________________________
4. ______________________________
5. ______________________________

Rate your happiness on a scale of 1 to 10: ______

If you are at a 6 or above, well done on making yourself happy!

If 5 or below, what else could you do to make yourself happy right now?

____

____

____

____

____

How do you feel (use a feeling word, like "mad," "sad," "bad," "glad," "afraid," "tired," or "hungry")? ____________________

What do you want? ______________________________

Desires

1. ____
2. ____
3. ____
4. ____
5. ____

Desires to Express

____

____

____

Receiving

What You Received:	How You Responded:
1. ____________	1. ____________
2. ____________	2. ____________
3. ____________	3. ____________
4. ____________	4. ____________
5. ____________	5. ____________

Gratitude

Daily Gratitude for Your Husband:	Expressed to Him?
1. ____________________	_____
2. ____________________	_____
3. ____________________	_____
4. ____________________	_____
5. ____________________	_____

Spouse-Fulfilling Prophecy

____

____

____

____

____

Evidence That Your Spouse-Fulfilling Prophecy Is True

1. ______________________________________

2. ______________________________________

3. ______________________________________

4. ______________________________________

5. ______________________________________

Day 24

How are you winning with the Six Intimacy Skills?

1. ______________________________
____

2. ______________________________
____

3. ______________________________
____

Self-Care

1. ______________________________
2. ______________________________
3. ______________________________
4. ______________________________
5. ______________________________

Rate your happiness on a scale of 1 to 10: ______

If you are at a 6 or above, well done on making yourself happy!

If 5 or below, what else could you do to make yourself happy right now?

____

____

____

____

____

How do you feel (use a feeling word, like "mad," "sad," "bad," "glad," "afraid," "tired," or "hungry")? ________________

What do you want? ____________________________

Desires

1. ____________________________________
2. ____________________________________
3. ____________________________________
4. ____________________________________
5. ____________________________________

Desires to Express

____

____

____

Receiving

What You Received:	How You Responded:
1. ________________	*1.* ________________
2. ________________	*2.* ________________
3. ________________	*3.* ________________
4. ________________	*4.* ________________
5. ________________	*5.* ________________

Gratitude

Daily Gratitude for Your Husband:	Expressed to Him?
1. ____________________________	______
2. ____________________________	______
3. ____________________________	______
4. ____________________________	______
5. ____________________________	______

Spouse-Fulfilling Prophecy

____

____

____

____

____

Evidence That Your Spouse-Fulfilling Prophecy Is True

1. ______________________________
2. ______________________________
3. ______________________________
4. ______________________________
5. ______________________________

Day 25

How are you winning with the Six Intimacy Skills?

1. ______________________________________

____

2. ______________________________________

____

3. ______________________________________

____

Self-Care

1. ______________________________________
2. ______________________________________
3. ______________________________________
4. ______________________________________
5. ______________________________________

Rate your happiness on a scale of 1 to 10: ______

If you are at a 6 or above, well done on making yourself happy!

If 5 or below, what else could you do to make yourself happy right now?

____

____

____

____

____

How do you feel (use a feeling word, like "mad," "sad," "bad," "glad," "afraid," "tired," or "hungry")? ______________

What do you want? ______________________

Desires

1. ______________________
2. ______________________
3. ______________________
4. ______________________
5. ______________________

Desires to Express

____

____

____

Receiving

What You Received:	How You Responded:
1. ________________	1. ________________
2. ________________	2. ________________
3. ________________	3. ________________
4. ________________	4. ________________
5. ________________	5. ________________

Gratitude

Daily Gratitude for Your Husband:	Expressed to Him?
1. ____________________________	______
2. ____________________________	______
3. ____________________________	______
4. ____________________________	______
5. ____________________________	______

Spouse-Fulfilling Prophecy

____

____

____

____

____

Evidence That Your Spouse-Fulfilling Prophecy Is True

1. ____
2. ____
3. ____
4. ____
5. ____

Day 26

How are you winning with the Six Intimacy Skills?

1. ______________________________

____

2. ______________________________

____

3. ______________________________

____

Self-Care

1. ______________________________
2. ______________________________
3. ______________________________
4. ______________________________
5. ______________________________

Rate your happiness on a scale of 1 to 10: ______

If you are at a 6 or above, well done on making yourself happy!

If 5 or below, what else could you do to make yourself happy right now?

____

____

____

____

____

How do you feel (use a feeling word, like "mad," "sad," "bad," "glad," "afraid," "tired," or "hungry")? ______________

What do you want? ______________________

Desires

1. ______________________
2. ______________________
3. ______________________
4. ______________________
5. ______________________

Desires to Express

____

____

____

Receiving

What You Received:	How You Responded:
1. ________________	*1.* ________________
2. ________________	*2.* ________________
3. ________________	*3.* ________________
4. ________________	*4.* ________________
5. ________________	*5.* ________________

Gratitude

Daily Gratitude for Your Husband:	Expressed to Him?
1. ____________________________	______
2. ____________________________	______
3. ____________________________	______
4. ____________________________	______
5. ____________________________	______

Spouse-Fulfilling Prophecy

____

____

____

____

____

Evidence That Your Spouse-Fulfilling Prophecy Is True

1. ____
2. ____
3. ____
4. ____
5. ____

Day 27

How are you winning with the Six Intimacy Skills?

1. ______________________________
____
2. ______________________________
____
3. ______________________________
____

Self-Care

1. ______________________________
2. ______________________________
3. ______________________________
4. ______________________________
5. ______________________________

Rate your happiness on a scale of 1 to 10: ______

If you are at a 6 or above, well done on making yourself happy!

If 5 or below, what else could you do to make yourself happy right now?

____

____

____

____

____

How do you feel (use a feeling word, like "mad," "sad," "bad," "glad," "afraid," "tired," or "hungry")? ____________________

What do you want? ______________________________

Desires

1. ____
2. ____
3. ____
4. ____
5. ____

Desires to Express

____

____

____

Receiving

What You Received:		How You Responded:	
1.	____________	*1.*	____________
2.	____________	*2.*	____________
3.	____________	*3.*	____________
4.	____________	*4.*	____________
5.	____________	*5.*	____________

Gratitude

Daily Gratitude for Your Husband:		Expressed to Him?
1.	________________________	______
2.	________________________	______
3.	________________________	______
4.	________________________	______
5.	________________________	______

Spouse-Fulfilling Prophecy

____

____

____

____

____

Evidence That Your Spouse-Fulfilling Prophecy Is True

1. ____
2. ____
3. ____
4. ____
5. ____

Day 28

How are you winning with the Six Intimacy Skills?

1. ______________________________

____

2. ______________________________

____

3. ______________________________

____

Self-Care

1. ______________________________
2. ______________________________
3. ______________________________
4. ______________________________
5. ______________________________

Rate your happiness on a scale of 1 to 10: ______

If you are at a 6 or above, well done on making yourself happy!

If 5 or below, what else could you do to make yourself happy right now?

____

____

____

____

____

How do you feel (use a feeling word, like "mad," "sad," "bad," "glad," "afraid," "tired," or "hungry")? ____________________

What do you want? ______________________________

Desires

1. ____
2. ____
3. ____
4. ____
5. ____

Desires to Express

____

____

____

Receiving

What You Received:	How You Responded:
1. ______________	*1.* ______________
2. ______________	*2.* ______________
3. ______________	*3.* ______________
4. ______________	*4.* ______________
5. ______________	*5.* ______________

Gratitude

Daily Gratitude for Your Husband:	Expressed to Him?
1. ______________________________	______
2. ______________________________	______
3. ______________________________	______
4. ______________________________	______
5. ______________________________	______

Spouse-Fulfilling Prophecy

____

____

____

____

____

Evidence That Your Spouse-Fulfilling Prophecy Is True

1. ____________________________________
2. ____________________________________
3. ____________________________________
4. ____________________________________
5. ____________________________________

Day 29

How are you winning with the Six Intimacy Skills?

1. ______________________________

____

2. ______________________________

____

3. ______________________________

____

Self-Care

1. ______________________________
2. ______________________________
3. ______________________________
4. ______________________________
5. ______________________________

Rate your happiness on a scale of 1 to 10: ______

If you are at a 6 or above, well done on making yourself happy!

If 5 or below, what else could you do to make yourself happy right now?

____

____

____

____

____

How do you feel (use a feeling word, like "mad," "sad," "bad," "glad," "afraid," "tired," or "hungry")? ________________

What do you want? ______________________________

Desires

1. ______________________________________
2. ______________________________________
3. ______________________________________
4. ______________________________________
5. ______________________________________

Desires to Express

____

____

____

Receiving

What You Received:	How You Responded:
1. ________________	1. ________________
2. ________________	2. ________________
3. ________________	3. ________________
4. ________________	4. ________________
5. ________________	5. ________________

Gratitude

Daily Gratitude for Your Husband:	Expressed to Him?
1. ________________________________	______
2. ________________________________	______
3. ________________________________	______
4. ________________________________	______
5. ________________________________	______

Spouse-Fulfilling Prophecy

____

____

____

____

____

Evidence That Your Spouse-Fulfilling Prophecy Is True

1. ____
2. ____
3. ____
4. ____
5. ____

Day 30

How are you winning with the Six Intimacy Skills?

1. ______________________________

   ____

2. ______________________________

   ____

3. ______________________________

   ____

Self-Care

1. ______________________________
2. ______________________________
3. ______________________________
4. ______________________________
5. ______________________________

Rate your happiness on a scale of 1 to 10: ______

If you are at a 6 or above, well done on making yourself happy!

If 5 or below, what else could you do to make yourself happy right now?

____

____

____

____

____

How do you feel (use a feeling word, like "mad," "sad," "bad," "glad," "afraid," "tired," or "hungry")? ______________

What do you want? ______________________

Desires

1. ______________________________________

2. ______________________________________

3. ______________________________________

4. ______________________________________

5. ______________________________________

Desires to Express

____

____

____

Receiving

What You Received:	How You Responded:
1. ________________	*1.* ________________
2. ________________	*2.* ________________
3. ________________	*3.* ________________
4. ________________	*4.* ________________
5. ________________	*5.* ________________

Gratitude

Daily Gratitude for Your Husband:	Expressed to Him?
1. ______________________________	______
2. ______________________________	______
3. ______________________________	______
4. ______________________________	______
5. ______________________________	______

Spouse-Fulfilling Prophecy

____

____

____

____

____

Evidence That Your Spouse-Fulfilling Prophecy Is True

1. ____________________________________
2. ____________________________________
3. ____________________________________
4. ____________________________________
5. ____________________________________

Insights and "A-ha!" Moments

Insights and "A-ha!" Moments

Insights and "A-ha!" Moments

Insights and "A-ha!" Moments

Insights and "A-ha!" Moments

Insights and "A-ha!" Moments

Insights and "A-ha!" Moments

Insights and "A-ha!" Moments

Insights and "A-ha!" Moments

Insights and "A-ha!" Moments

About the Author

Laura Doyle is a *New York Times* bestselling author, marriage expert, and the founder of Laura Doyle Connect, an international relationship coaching school that certifies coaches and guides students in practicing The Six Intimacy Skills™ to make their marriages last and thrive.

Her books are translated into nineteen languages and published in thirty countries. Laura is also the host of *The Empowered Wife Podcast* and the *Empowered Wives TV* series on Amazon Prime. She is on a mission to end world divorce.

She has appeared on *CBS Evening News*, *Dateline NBC*, *The Today Show*, *Good Morning America*, and *The View*. She has been featured in the *Wall Street Journal*, the *New York Times*, the *Los Angeles Times*, the *Washington Post*, the *London Telegraph*, and the *New Yorker*.

But the thing she's most proud of is her playful, passionate, thirty-three-year marriage with her hilarious husband, John, who has been dressing himself since before she was born.